NATIONAL GEOGRAPHIC

M000192418

We're Going Camping

Sarah Russell

We're going camping.
We'll be spending two nights in the woods.
We'll need to take everything we need,
including shelter, food, and supplies.

There aren't any houses in the woods.
Where will we stay?

3

We'll pitch a tent and sleep in it.
The tent is light and easy to carry.
The tent is made out of a material
that repels water.
It will keep us dry if it rains.

There aren't any stores in the woods.
What will we eat?

We'll take all the food we need with us.
We'll also take a cook stove.
The cook stove is light and easy to carry.
We can use it to cook our food.
We'll take plates, cups, and utensils, too.

There aren't any beds in the woods.
What will we sleep on?

We'll take sleeping bags and sleep in them.
The sleeping bags are light and easy to carry.
The sleeping bags are made out of
a material that will keep us warm.

**There isn't any electricity in the woods.
How will we see at night?**

We'll take a flashlight.
A flashlight is light and easy to carry.
A flashlight runs on batteries.
A flashlight will help us see in the dark.

What will we do when we're camping?

We'll have fun!